Original title:
Sage Sayings

Copyright © 2025 Creative Arts Management OÜ
All rights reserved.

Author: Evelyn Hartman
ISBN HARDBACK: 978-1-80566-736-0
ISBN PAPERBACK: 978-1-80566-865-7

Cultivating Awareness

In the garden of thought, weeds can creep,
Pull them out gently, don't lose sleep.
Mind's a patchwork of laughs and sighs,
Watch out for thoughts that wear funny ties.

Notice the clouds, some float like a boat,
Others just hang like an old, worn coat.
Joy in the chaos, a tip from the wise,
Life's a circus, grab a clown's surprise!

The Dance of Discernment

Life's a dance floor, but watch your feet,
Step on the toes of truths bittersweet.
Twirl with the facts, shimmy with flair,
Make a mistake? Just act like you care!

Some truths wear sneakers, some wear a gown,
Pick the wrong partner, you'll fall on down.
But hey! Get up, and try out a dip,
Life's too short, let laughter equip!

Whispers of Wisdom

Wisdom sometimes wears an old baseball cap,
It throws you a line, then laughs at the map.
If you trip on a saying, just wave and grin,
The punchline is here, let the fun begin!

Listen closely, the whispers are sly,
They sneak up like cats, oh my, oh my!
Don't take it too serious, give it a whirl,
Life's just a joke, in a wild, sweet swirl!

The Echo of Experience

Experience chuckles, a mischievous dude,
He shows you the stuff that's mostly crude.
Like a rubber chicken that honks by your side,
It takes all kinds of wits for this ride!

So when echoes call, don't hide or retreat,
They've got punchlines tucked in just for your beat.
Remember each story's a chance to derive,
A giggle, a snort, and truly feel alive!

Beneath the Elder Tree

Beneath the elder tree we sit,
With wise old roots and tales that fit.
A squirrel tells jokes, all nuts and glee,
"Don't climb too high, you might lose your spree!"

The shadows dance as stories flow,
Life's lessons wrapped in a humorous show.
Old leaves whisper and giggle, it's true,
"Life's a jest; eat dessert first, then stew!"

Lanterns of Legacy

Lanterns flicker with wisdom bright,
Each glow a chuckle, a tiny delight.
A flicked switch brings tales from the past,
"Remember to laugh, life races fast!"

In each warm beam, a lesson glows,
"Wear mismatched socks; nobody knows!"
Old lamps chuckle with each gentle sway,
"Join the dance; let worries stray!"

The Tapestry of Thought

Threads of thought weave funny designs,
With patterns of laughter and playful lines.
"Don't take it seriously," the wise ones quip,
"Life's a rollercoaster; just enjoy the trip!"

We patch together joys, and oh, what a sight,
"Forget the diet; eat cake each night!"
Each knot tells tales of folly and cheer,
"Why fit in the mold? Yuletide's near!"

Seasons of Sagacity

In spring, wisdom blooms with sass,
"A shovel's for dirt, not for class!"
Summer's sun brings laughter galore,
"Take a nap, life's too much to explore!"

Autumn leaves rustle with giggles and grins,
"Don't rake too much; it's all in the spins!"
Winter wraps up with a cozy cheer,
"Hot cocoa cures all; that's the frontier!"

Musings from the Mountain

On the mountain high, I thought I'd find,
Wisdom wrapped in clouds, of the quirky kind.
But the crows laughed loud, and the goats declared,
"Come take a hike, if you aren't scared!"

The rocks whispered tales, of times long past,
As squirrels chased shadows, oh what a blast!
With every wise crack, the peaks echoed back,
'Nature's punchlines are never off track!'

Voices Beneath the Surface

Down by the stream, I eavesdropped keen,
Fish gossiping secrets, oh what a scene!
They winked and they splashed, in a watery jest,
"Here's our tip: never dry, take life as a fest!"

The frogs croaked a tune about life's little quirks,
A chorus of chuckles, from muddy works.
They lured in the flies, with their slippery charm,
'Life's a big joke, just don't take up arms!'

Insights from the Ages

Old trees gave a nod as I pondered their bark,
"You'll find wisdom's glow in the light after dark.
Just wear your shades and don't trip on roots,
Life's silly enough without wearing boots!"

The stones chimed along with a hearty laugh,
"It's better to tumble than stay on the path!
Let your heart be light, like a feather in flight,
And don't take it too serious, it's all just delight!"

The Cultivation of Thought

In the garden of mind, I planted a seed,
With water and laughter, it started to breed.
The weeds whispered gently, 'We're part of the play,
Embrace us with humor, you'll find a bright way!'

Sunshine giggled down, on the blooms all around,
While bees buzzed sweet secrets, without making a sound.

'Life's a tangled vine, but each twist is a cheer,
So prune away worries, and let joy steer!'

Fireflies of Insight

In the dark, they flicker bright,
Guiding thoughts like stars at night.
A dance of wisdom in the air,
Glowing quirks show they care.

Chasing shadows, they play tricks,
Bouncing off the mind's quick flicks.
With laughter in each glowing blink,
You'll find the truths you never think.

So catch a glow, embrace the jest,
In the light, you find your best.
For every laugh can shine a light,
On thoughts that make your heart take flight.

The Canvas of Experience

Life's a canvas, wild and bright,
Splashes of color, a funny sight.
Each stroke tells tales, both good and bad,
A masterpiece of silly and mad.

Sometimes it drips, sometimes it spills,
Each mistake brings hearty thrills.
Mix the blues with a pinch of red,
Laughter and wisdom wrap your head.

So paint away, don't hold back,
Joy resides in every crack.
From smudges to strokes that fly,
Find humor where the colors lie.

Echoes of Elation

In whispers soft, the laughs resound,
Echoes of joy can always be found.
While stumbles trip our happy feet,
Laughter makes each moment sweet.

Tickles of truth bounce off the walls,
In every giggle, life enthralls.
Let your heart sing, let it soar,
Through echoes, find what's worth living for.

So, dance and shout with wild delight,
Elation's glow is always right.
In life's grand hall, hear the calls,
The echoing laughter never stalls.

Tales from the Timeworn

Old folks chuckle with wisdom shared,
Crafty quips, a heart prepared.
With tales of yore, they spin their yarn,
In laughter, life's lessons are born.

Nostalgia drips like honey sweet,
Each story told, impossible to beat.
Through winks and nods, they sprinkle cheer,
Turning fables to laugh with dear.

Gather round for the wisdom bytes,
In every tale, a spirit ignites.
For in the old, the young will see,
Fun is steeped in history.

Phrases from the Past

Once they said, 'Don't count your chicks,
There's always a fox with its tricks.'
So I keep my eggs in a safe little nook,
And I just stick to my cookbook.

Old folks say that laughter's the cure,
But they forget where they placed their hearing, I'm sure.
If wisdom comes with age, I must confess,
I still can't find my socks, more or less.

With every wrinkle, there's a grin,
A reminder of trouble just waiting to begin.
They say time flies, but I think it hides,
Behind my glasses, along for the rides.

Dinner's best when your guests are like wine,
The older the better, the better the time.
So raise a toast to the phrases that last,
And let's laugh together, forgetting the past.

Voices of the Aged

The wise man said, 'Don't judge a book,
Till you've seen it with a good old look.'
But I just squint, 'cause the print's too small,
And I've lost my place at the last chapter's call.

'A stitch in time saves nine,' they say,
But I'm using duct tape to get through the day.
With every fix, there's a funny mishap,
Like mixing my soup with my cat's new cap.

'An apple a day keeps the doctor away,'
But I'd rather have cake—what do they say?
They laugh at my choices, my snacks, my jokes,
But they're the ones turning to easy-to-fix hoax.

So here's to the elders, full of good cheer,
With each pointless nugget, they spread the weird.
In a world that spins faster than ever before,
I'll take their advice and still eat cake galore.

Ancient Words, Modern Hearts

They say, 'A penny saved is a penny earned,'
But I spent mine all just for fun, I learned.
With wallets so light, we dance through the store,
It's my wallet's fault, not my spending rapport!

When life gives you lemons, go make a pie,
But I've got a feeling I'll just let them dry.
The wisdom of ages, packed up with glee,
Makes me chuckle when fruit flies are free!

Old folks love to share their nuggets of truth,
Tales from the past that still turn out uncouth.
But maybe I'll listen and take some advice,
As long as it doesn't come sprinkled with spice!

'You can't teach an old dog new tricks,' they say,
But I saw mine hula hoop just yesterday.
So let's keep our hearts light, our laughter alive,
With ancient advice, we'll take a good dive!

Timeless Truths

'Too many cooks spoil the broth,' they home,
But I just want food! Make it from my phone!
With delivery men bringing me all of my dreams,
I'm the chef of the kitchen that nobody redeems.

'Don't put all your eggs in one basket,' they warn,
But I brought a picnic, so let my heart mourn.
For the baskets are shiny, the eggs are quite crack,
And my lunch invitation may need to retract.

They say, 'Good things come to those who wait,'
But I'm tapping my foot, losing all sense of fate.
For patience is virtue—maybe it's true,
But my pizza's arriving at a quarter past two!

So let's raise our glasses to tips of the wise,
While we munch on our snacks and create our own highs.
The truths may be timeless, but laughter is key,
Let's keep chatting and chuckling; come share some with me!

Wisdom in the Shadows

In the dark where wisdom hides,
A sock's lost, but the truth abides.
Tread lightly, don't wake the cat,
For fortune favors the odd and fat.

Chickens cross for reasons unknown,
While gossip thrives on ancient phone.
When life hands you lemons, take a bite,
Sour zest makes everything bright.

A wise old owl once said in jest,
'When in doubt, just wear a vest!'
For style can mask a clueless fate,
And laughter makes the silly great.

Fragments of Familiarity

The ants march on in organized lines,
While we humans spend time on wine.
In the fridge, leftovers mold and grow,
'Last week's dinner? A fine no-show!'

When someone advises you to relax,
Remember the time they lost their snacks.
Their wisdom wrapped in double cheese,
Is best consumed with a side of pleas.

The kettle sings, then forgets the flip,
Advice is like tea—it needs a sip.
Pour it hot, or it turns to ice,
But sometimes, burnt tea is just as nice.

The Poetry of Experience

A shoe on the wrong foot, mischief untold,
They say learn from love, but it's still on hold.
With each failed date, a lesson rings true,
'Always ask which side the dog will chew!'

Life is a dance with two left feet,
And every misstep makes it sweet.
So twirl and spin, embrace the fall,
For experience laughs after all.

In searching for gold, misfortune we find,
Strange treasures of the oddest kind.
So savor the trips of blunders divine,
Remember, life's a joke—it's all by design.

Heritage in a Whisper

Grandma's wisdom, wrapped in pie crust,
'Knead life with love, in flour we trust.'
With every roll, and pinch of salt,
A family recipe, humor's the vault.

Stories told near a flickering flame,
'How your uncle danced—what a shame!'
With laughter echoing through the night,
Heritage shines in the silliest light.

Old photos show us back in the day,
Where mustaches ruled in a goofy display.
In every frame, a chuckle hides,
For life's a jest that time confides.

The Art of Listening

If you speak while I'm chewing, you lose the debate,
You can't win an argument with a mouthful of plate.
So I nod and I smile, while thoughts drift away,
And plot my next snack for a glorious day.

Listen close, my friend, while you eat your pie,
The wisdom's all there, just don't ask me why.
With a crumb on my lip and a wink from my eye,
I'll mix up my munchies with a wink and a sigh.

Roots of Resilience

When life hands you lemons, just add some gin,
Shake things up a bit, let the fun times begin.
For every setback faced, find a joke to share,
A chuckle can turn burdens into thin air.

So if you trip and fall, do a dance on the floor,
Embrace every tumble, you'll soon find the score.
Life's a comedy show, wear a laughable grin,
With roots deep in joy, let the resilience win.

A Journey in Reflection

Stand in front of mirrors, and what do you see?
Just a face full of puns and a goofy old me.
Reflecting on choices, they shimmer and sway,
Like a funhouse of thoughts, it's a wild cabaret.

Every glance back, there's a giggle to find,
Lessons learned in sideways, with humor aligned.
So chuckle at errors, let the past give a cheer,
A journey in laughter is the path we hold dear.

The Silence Speaks

In a room full of chatter, I find it is clear,
That silence can sing like a tune in your ear.
With a pause for the punchline, and a wink of delight,
Sometimes the quiet just gets it just right.

So when words take a vacation, let stillness abound,
In the hush, you may hear laughter echo around.
With silence as my partner, together we play,
In the symphony of peace, every joke finds its way.

Chasing Shadows of Insight

In whispers, wisdom haunts the air,
Like cats that know just when to stare.
The less you know, the more you learn,
So at the pot, just let it burn.

A broken clock can still be right,
Especially when it's dark at night.
Dance with fools, they lead the way,
To fortunes that are here to stay.

The road to truth is much too long,
Yet every twist helps you feel strong.
Plato said, under a tree,
"This isn't what it's cracked up to be!"

Take heed, my friend, when laughter flies,
For often wisdom wears a guise.
Stumble and fall, just laugh it off,
The secret's in the jester's scoff.

Verses from the Elders

Grandpa said with eyes so bright,
"Don't be shy, it's quite alright."
When life gives lemons, make a pie,
And always dream beyond the sky.

A wise old crone once had a thought,
"The perfect plan was never caught."
So chase your goals like a spinning top,
Just don't forget to make a stop.

In riddles deep, the truth resides,
But who can solve when laughter hides?
"Love your pets, they'll love you back,"
Was all she said, then off she'll pack.

The years creep by like creeping fog,
So make your mark, you clever dog!
With every quip and silly jest,
You'll find that life can be the best!

The Path of Perception

Walk the path with muddy shoes,
For every step, there's much to lose.
The wise man grins with playful eyes,
"Don't take life too seriously, it lies!"

Pick up the crumbs that laughter drops,
And dance like no one ever stops.
The weight of wisdom's quite the chore,
So trade it in for something more!

Beneath the grins, the truth will hide,
So roll the dice and take that ride.
In silly dreams, the brightest glows,
As clumsy steps may lead to shows.

So tread lightly, joy is found,
In every silly, happy sound.
Skip ahead, don't count your years,
Life's a joke, so shift your gears!

Gems of the Past

From ancient scrolls of giggles come,
A simple truth that makes us hum.
"Sometimes you win, and sometimes you lose,
Just wear your socks and baby shoes."

In halls of laughter, echoes gleam,
Reminding us to chase a dream.
The past is but a playful prank,
So when in doubt, just laugh, then tank!

Old wise tales cannot be tamed,
When life seems tough, they've been blamed.
So wear your joy like a crown so bright,
For laughter cures the darkest night.

And gather now these charming gems,
For life is better with some friends.
When in doubt, just wink and sway,
Make fun of life, come what may!

Threads in the Tapestry

Weaves of wisdom, tangled tight,
A fable spun in morning light.
The yarn of truths, they twist and twirl,
Knots of laughter in each swirl.

A sock could be a hat, no doubt,
And still we wear it, all about!
If life gives lemons, make some pie,
Then eat it quick before you cry.

Patterns silly, stories bold,
Each thread a tale, a jest retold.
In this fabric, joy's the seam,
We stitch it up, live out our dream.

When Shadows Speak

In the evening, shadows prance,
Whispering secrets, taking a chance.
They might say, 'Don't take a fall,'
Or just hint, 'Don't eat that last meatball!'

When they chuckle, it's quite absurd,
They tell the tales without a word.
So sidestep drama, with a grin,
And dance along, let the games begin!

Their voices echo, teasingly near,
Always reminding, don't take life severe.
With mischief brewing in the night,
We'll laugh 'til dawn, till morning light.

The Notes of Nostalgia

Oh, the tunes that tickle the ear,
Bring laughter back, bring joy and cheer.
Old vinyl spins a quirky tale,
Of socks mismatched, of treasure trails.

The past can dance in wild delight,
With hiccuped dreams and wonky flight.
Let's toast to all those silly lines,
That shaped our lives like crooked signs.

The notes that flutter through our minds,
Are but reminders of what one finds.
In laughter's rhythm, we shall sway,
Nostalgia's game, come out and play!

Harvest of Humility

In the garden, pride's a weed,
Choke it out; it's not a seed.
Pumpkins grow from humble ground,
While foolish onions tumble down.

Pick the apples, nice and round,
Laughter's fruit is truly found.
For every boast, there's one to share,
With humor's hand, debonair.

So gather 'round, the harvest's here,
We share our flaws, while sipping beer.
With giggles sprouting all around,
In humble joy, true grace is found.

Proverbs in the Breeze

A bird in the hand, or so they say,
Just don't let it poop on your way!
Laugh at your troubles, let them be light,
Tomorrow might bring a whimsical flight.

Two heads are better, but double the mess,
Arguments usually lead to distress.
If a penny saved is never spent,
Then what's the fun? Only time to lament!

Don't count your chickens before they hatch,
Especially when you can't find a match.
The grass is greener, it's surely a tease,
Unless you get stuck in some sticky cheese!

So live life simply, with joy and with glee,
And don't let the world put a frown on thee.
For laughter and joy, they're the best in the end,
A good joke is worth more than a good friend!

The Wisdom We Carry

When life gives you lemons, throw them away,
Just like mom said at the end of the day.
A watched pot never boils, that's quite true,
But I've seen kettle dances - how about you?

Curiosity killed the cat, that's a fact,
But satisfaction brought it right back.
If at first you don't succeed, try and try,
And if that fails, let out a big sigh!

You can't teach an old dog new tricks, they say,
But perhaps he just needs a good run and play.
Better late than never, but early's quite neat,
So roll out of bed, don't accept defeat!

Keep your friends close, your snacks even nearer,
For food is the fuel, and laughter's the clearer.
So walk through this life with a grin and a quip,
And you'll find joy riding on your ship!

Echoes of the Ancients

An ounce of prevention's worth more than a pound,
Just ask your shoes when they hit the ground.
The early bird catches more than just worms,
But those sleeping in don't care for terms.

If you can't stand the heat, get out of the kitchen,
Or grab a cold drink, that's a smart mission!
Many hands make light work, they insist,
But who's making the sandwiches? Come, take your list!

Time flies when you're having fun, oh so true,
But it also trips when you're stuck in a queue.
A penny for your thoughts? That's a steal,
Let's negotiate dinner, what's your ideal meal?

So here's to the wisdom that makes life a ride,
With laughter and quirks, let joy be your guide.
For in echoes of ancients, lessons unfold,
But it's the stories we live that are worth more than gold!

Through the Lens of Time

Haste makes waste; that's something to heed,
But please don't call me if you're in need!
Don't put all your eggs in one basket way high,
Unless you've got wings, then give it a try.

Too many cooks spoil the broth, oh dear,
Just don't blame the chef when it's burned here.
If the shoe fits, wear it; that's awfully nice,
But what if it's pink? At least it's precise!

You reap what you sow, that's a famous line,
But if you sow daisies, you might feel divine!
If life's a bowl of cherries, pick wisely,
Or you might end up with pits that surprise thee!

So take all this wisdom, add humor and cheer,
And let laughter's melody sing in your ear.
Through the lens of time, we'll dance and we'll rhyme,
For fun in our journey makes every hour chime!

Lanterns of Insight

Bright ideas flicker like flames,
Chasing shadows, playing games.
A peek inside the noodle box,
Watch out for those brainy flocks!

Wisdom comes dressed up in quirks,
Like a cat that always lurks.
Laughing lessons fill the air,
With a wink and a silly stare.

Bumbling thoughts can lead the way,
Just ask the squirrels at play.
Rusty old minds seek fresh cheese,
And steal the thoughts with such great ease!

So grab a light, don't take too long,
Find wisdom in a silly song.
Each twinkle shines with laughter's roar,
Who knew learning could be such a chore?

Ancestral Echoes

Old tales whispered through the trees,
Carried on a playful breeze.
Great Aunt Edna cracks a joke,
About the time her cat once spoke.

Grandpa's wisdom, chuckles wrapped,
Said, 'If you trip, just take a nap!'
With every tale, a grin appears,
'Don't worry, it's just silly fears!'

Footsteps echo on the floor,
Ancestors giggle, wanting more.
Life's a dance, a funny spree,
With lessons tucked in jokes so free.

To snort with laughter or just sigh,
As wisdom's feathers take to fly.
In every hiccup, there's a spark,
Trust your gut—just leave a mark!

Reflections of the Wise

Mirrors crack with quirky truths,
Jumbled thoughts of silly youths.
The wise can laugh at their own blunders,
As wisdom hides in playful wonders.

With each fumble and stuttered line,
They dance through life, sipping wine.
Best advice comes through a grin,
Like falling flat but still wearing skin.

Bright ideas float in fluffy hats,
A wise old owl on silly spats.
With every riddle that we weave,
Remember, life is meant to leave.

Gather laughter, spread the cheer,
For wisdom sharpens with each beer.
So raise a toast to blunders sweet,
Chuckles nestled where wisdom meets!

Clouds of Knowledge

Fluffy thoughts drift up above,
Filled with giggles and some love.
Each puffy cloud has tales to share,
But watch out—don't get caught in their snare!

Mistakes rain down like sunny sprinkles,
Turning frowns into happy twinkles.
Float on dreams, let them collide,
In a whirlwind, let wisdom ride.

Stormy thoughts can make you blink,
But laughter's the final link.
So grab your thoughts, toss 'em high,
Dance through life as clouds float by.

With every giggle that spills from the sky,
Our minds grow light, and dreams can fly.
Finding joy in each silly phrase,
Is how we navigate through life's maze!

The Pluck of Phrases

Wise words can tickle the ear,
Laughter often hides near.
A jest from the wise old chap,
Will turn a frown into a clap.

In every quirk, there's a clue,
The best advice may sound askew.
Like socks that never match,
Life's oddities are quite the catch.

When fortune calls, don't be shy,
Grab the phone, let laughter fly.
A pickle's just a cucumber's ride,
If you dress it up with pride.

So take a hint, don't be sad,
A chuckle's the best gift you've had.
For when life throws a curveball your way,
Just laugh, and let the wisdom play.

Quotations from Quietude

In the silence, whispers creep,
Nuggets of wisdom, oh so deep.
A snore can hide a wise old thought,
Even while battling sleep you've fought.

Chasing dreams can make you tumble,
But joy is found in every stumble.
A clumsy dance speaks volumes true,
Even if your two left feet construe.

When in doubt, just wear a hat,
It's not magic, but hey, how 'bout that?
Life's a riddle, with laughs galore,
So grab a pun and dance some more.

Find humor in things mundane,
For wisdom grows from a little pain.
A laugh shared is trouble halved,
With jests and jibes, may your heart be salved.

A Symphony of Sentiments

From the archives of the heart,
Comes a tune, a quirky part.
When life's a song, hum along,
Sing with joy, you can't go wrong.

Epiphanies in the oddest places,
Can bring giggles to your faces.
A rubber chicken might just be,
The truth you're searching for, you see?

So tip your hat to fate's embrace,
And dance like no one's in the race.
For wisdom's found in playful jest,
With laughter, you'll outshine the best.

Tales of woe were meant to amuse,
In every blunder, there's a muse.
Take heed, my friend, and don't despair,
The symphony of life is always there.

The Elders' Almanac

In the land of wrinkles and gray,
Lies wisdom dressed in humor's play.
A nod and wink from the weathered cheek,
Will make the finest lessons speak.

When life seems scripted and quite absurd,
Recall the wit in every word.
A pie in the face may seem misplaced,
But laughter lingers, life's sweet grace.

A riddle wrapped in a grandparent's sway,
Holds secrets that will brighten your day.
So steal a moment, pause to grin,
The almanac of laughs begins within.

Amidst the tales and sunlit dreams,
Are bits of wisdom that burst at the seams.
So gather 'round and share a jest,
In laughter, dear friends, we are truly blessed.

The Relics of Rhetoric

Words can dance and play the fool,
In jest, they sharpen every tool.
A witty quip, a playful jest,
Brings laughter forth, it's for the best.

A clever line can turn the tide,
Where wisdom walks, jokes often hide.
To giggle at the serious stuff,
Is the way to say, life's enough.

In jokes, there lies a secret key,
Unlocking thoughts, so wild and free.
When life gets rough, just take a seat,
And wear your humor like a treat.

So gather 'round and lend an ear,
For wisecracks whispered, that we cheer.
From olden times, the laughter rings,
As ancient wisdom winks and sings.

Bedtime Stories from the Wise

Once upon a midnight clear,
The wise old owl shared, "Never fear!
When life's a mess, just give a grin,
For joy is where the fun begins."

"Wear mismatched socks, it's quite a game!
And never let your hat feel shame.
Flip your frown, it's good advice,
Like adding sprinkles to your rice!"

"Don't count your sheep, count all the laughs,
For joy in life is how time drafts.
In every tale, find humor's charm,
To ward off worry, keep you warm."

As lights grew dim, the stories spun,
While sleepy smiles glimmered, one by one.
In winks and giggles, lay the theme,
Bedtime wisdom wraps like a dream.

The Whispering Winds of Ages

In breezes soft, wise words do tease,
With giggles found in rustling leaves.
They whisper tales of joy and jest,
Encouraging us to feel our best.

"Follow your dreams," the zephyrs croon,
"Except the one with a snoring raccoon!"
For every cloud that seems to frown,
There's laughter waiting, turn it around.

Listen close, for nature's gift,
In a chuckle's sway, we learn to lift.
Seek wisdom not in solemn tones,
But in the funny quirks life owns.

Let every gust bring forth a cheer,
And spin the tales that we hold dear.
For in the winds, both wise and free,
Lies laughter's touch, our remedy.

The Leaflet of Life Lessons

A leaf fell down with a wink and grin,
"Life's a dance, you join, not spin!
Tohoop in joy, while others fret,
Is how to laugh, you won't regret."

"Wear silly hats and dance in rain,
Find joy in glitches, sunshine, or pain.
When faced with frowns, just make a face,
And turn the heat into a race!"

Beneath the shade, wisdom's root,
Is laughter born from silly pursuit.
In every blunder, a lesson gleams,
Like chocolate sauce in sweet ice cream.

So gather up these gentle hints,
With jokes that stitch and life that glints.
Embrace the folly, hold it tight,
For laughter's warmth is pure delight.

Silent Guideposts

When life hands you lemons, just make a pie,
For laughter's the answer, oh me, oh my!
Don't take it too serious, it's part of the game,
A chuckle a day keeps you away from fame.

If the road seems too bumpy, just take a detour,
Silly signs ahead, saying laugh! – for sure!
Dance in the rain, don't worry, be spry,
Life's too short to worry about the why.

Wear mismatched socks, it's quite the new trend,
Let the world watch and giggle, it's fun to offend!
Ask ducks for advice, they quack like they know,
And remember, dear friend, it's all about flow.

So take every mishap with a wink and a smile,
Wear joy like a cape, it's totally worthwhile!
For laughter's the guidepost, a beacon so clear,
Follow the funny, and you'll steer good cheer.

Epiphanies of the Aged

Wisdom comes wrapped in a crinkly guise,
Like old cheese that's aged, or an onion's sweet prize.
The wrinkles are stories, they giggle and roam,
But remember, young friend, we all have a home.

The best advice given, with a wink and a grin,
Is to dance like no one's watching, even at din.
Seniors with sass, striking poses with flair,
A game of bingo can lead to fresh air!

Count every candle; they're friends in disguise,
Don't fret about age, just look at the prize.
With tea cups and laughter, we celebrate time,
Finding joy in the journey, oh isn't it prime?

So heed all the laughter from elders galore,
Their quirks are your treasure, promise you'll score!
Embrace every giggle, the quirks that they bring,
For the older we get, the more fun we fling.

Threads of Distillation

Life's a tapestry, frayed at the seams,
With threads made of blunders and whimsical dreams.
So sewing with laughter, we'll patch every tear,
With humor as fabric, it's fun to declare.

Take a sip from the cup filled with giggly grace,
For wisdom distilled often comes with a face.
The secret recipe? A dash of delight,
With a pinch of absurdity to brighten the night.

As we weave through the years with spots here and there,
Let's turn every mishap into sparkly flair!
With needles of kindness, we stitch up our fate,
In the quilt of our lives, may laughter await.

So gather your threads, let's create quite a show,
With color and laughter, a delight we will sow.
Through frolic and fun, life's tapestry gleams,
In the threads of our journey, we build up our dreams.

Echoing Melodies of Thought

In the orchestra of life, play the flute with a laugh,
Serenading the troubles, dismissing the chaff.
For melodies linger, they twirl in the air,
Echoing wisdom, but never a care.

With trumpets of silliness, let's march down the street,
Clapping to rhythms with wiggly feet.
When your thoughts go astray, let humor be found,
In the echoes of joy, let your spirit rebound.

So dance to the tunes, written by the breeze,
Finding harmony hidden in life's little keys.
For laughter's a chorus, it rises and swells,
In the concert of living, it softly compels.

With each note we share, our spirits unite,
Creating sweet symphonies, bathed in warm light.
So sing out your heart, let the melodies flow,
For in the echoes of laughter, true wisdom will grow.

Glimmers of Clarity

In the chaos of daily grind,
Wisdom's often hard to find.
A penny saved is a penny earned,
But who buys soup with pennies turned?

When life gives you lemons, squeeze 'em tight,
Then sell lemonade; that feels just right.
A stitch in time saves nine, they say,
But two stitches? That's just your pay!

If you can't find joy, make a mess,
Dance like nobody's watching, I guess.
To err is human, to laugh divine,
So let's embrace the wobbly line!

Plenty of fish? They swim away,
So bait your hook in a humorous way.
A fool and his money soon part true,
But if happiness costs, I'll bid you adieu!

The Language of Experience

Life's a comedy wrapped in pain,
Like socks that vanish in the rain.
With every expert comes a fool,
Juggling wisdom like a school.

To have a friend, be a little silly,
Make them laugh till it's truly frilly.
Laughter's a compass, it points the way,
Even if it leads you to a play!

Some chase the dream, some chase the cat,
But never chase a rumor; that's just flat!
When they say, 'Follow your heart', take the lead,
As long as it's not towards a stampeding steed!

With age comes laughs, although grey and worn,
Trust me, it's better than being forlorn.
So pour a glass of wisdom's brew,
And let the nonsense seep through!

Timeless Offerings

The early bird might get the worm,
But sleeping in? Comes with charm.
To err is human, to laugh a must,
So let's giggle at our own bust!

You catch more flies with honey, they say,
But who needs flies on a sunny day?
A rolling stone gathers no moss,
But it sure knows how to take a toss!

Life's a game, a quirky maze,
Where each decision warrants a gaze.
If you're stumbling, it's all in fun,
Just don't trip over the 'to-do' run!

At the end of the day, wear a grin,
For laughter adds warmth from within.
So share a chuckle, spread the light,
And dance around the joy tonight!

Beneath the Surface

Underneath the waves of thought,
Lies humor, bubbling as it ought.
When life gets heavy, float a while,
Turn the frown into a cheeky smile!

They say the truth will set you free,
But so does ice cream, trust in me!
Pickles in pies? A delightful twist,
In wisdom's book, it cannot be missed!

A watched pot never boils, it's true,
But if you dance, it might just brew!
So keep your worries light and breezy,
For laughter makes the hard days easy!

So here's to wisdom with a flair,
To joy and giggles that fill the air.
Dig deep for laughter, don't lose your nerve,
For life's a jester in its quirky curve!

Brushing Against the Bronzed Past

When wisdom turns a shade of gray,
The old folks laugh at the youthful fray.
With every tale they spin and weave,
You'll find more twists than you'd believe.

They'll sprinkle puns like breadcrumbs wide,
And nod as if they were the guide.
"Remember, child, a penny saved,
Is just a dime that never braved!"

Their stories drift like autumn leaves,
With punchlines hidden 'neath their eaves.
The more you listen, the less you know,
Life's riddle wrapped in a comical show.

So take their words, a side of jest,
In their wild lore, you'll find the best.
From golden years to giggles shared,
In every laugh, a truth declared.

The Lingering Light of Lore

When elders toss their jests like dice,
The wisdom's sweet, but oh, so nice!
Their tales, like socks, may come unwound,
Yet laughter's treasure can still be found.

In kitchens where the stories roast,
You'll find the punchlines matter most.
They'll poke fun at their youthful days,
While serving wisdom in quirky ways.

They declare, "Never trust a cat,
Unless you're sure it's just a brat!"
With every wink, a lesson blooms,
In between the cackles and the fumes.

So gather round, let humor rule,
For wise is who can laugh at fools.
From lingering light, the tales be spun,
To chase the clouds and find the sun.

Inked in the Soul

A tattoo here, a story there,
Each inked line full of myth and flair.
They say wisdom's best when dressed in fun,
Like ice cream on a summer run.

"Life's a canvas, so paint it bright,
Even if you spill the peach delight!"
As laughter echoes down the hall,
You'll find the truth in every sprawl.

From wise old owls, you get the scoop,
They offer tidbits in the loop.
"Just add a wink to spicy lore,
And see how wisdom starts to soar!"

With every giggle, ink does flow,
Into the heart where wisdom grows.
And when you find that silly grin,
You'll know the soul is inked within.

Heartstrings of Heritage

The tales of old go strumming 'round,
Like banjos in a lively crowd.
From granddad's chair to grandma's stew,
Laughter dances, a merry crew.

With every string tugged, echoes play,
The wisdom that won't fade away.
"Happiness! It's just a rhyme,
Put on your shoes and dance with time!"

So toss the weight of worldly woes,
In family lore, the humor glows.
Heartstrings strummed with love and jest,
In every giggle, you'll find the best.

So gather close, let stories ring,
With quirky tales, the heart takes wing.
Embrace the past with cheeky cheer,
For what's been sung, forever near.

Reflections of the Elders

Old folks say with glimmering eyes,
"Don't sweat the small stuff, eat the fries!"
Life's a dance, just twirl and sway,
But don't forget your laundry day.

With wisdom comes some quirky rhymes,
"Keep your teeth; they save you dimes!"
Better laughs than sharper minds,
In giggles, true magic one finds.

When storms arise and troubles creep,
"Just wear a hat and take a leap!"
With each fall, there's a chance to rise,
And snatch dessert—that's the prize!

So heed these tales we love to share,
"Don't touch the stove; it's quite a scare!"
In every jest, a lesson gleams,
Old souls know, it's not what it seems.

The Art of Knowing

In the world of wise and quirky prattle,
"You can't ride a cow, just pick a cattle!"
Ask questions, let your laugh out loud,
   Wisdom hides in a giggling crowd.

Listen close when the grandmas glow,
   "Never wrestle with a dog; just go!"
   Try to find joy in silly spree,
For laughter's art, is key to be free.

Each riddle hides a chuckle or two,
"You can't become a rock; you're not a shoe!"
Unlock your heart with playful wit,
   Truth often wears a wisecrack fit.

So tip your hat to those who jest,
"Make friends with squirrels; they're the best!"
For in this art, we dance and play,
Life's a punchline—we're here to stay.

Guided by the Generations

Grandparents joke as they knit away,
"Once lost my keys; they never stray!"
In tales of yore, there's laughter bright,
    Crazy antics bring pure delight.

A wise one says, with a wink so sly,
"Eat your greens, but pizza's nearby!"
    Life's a buffet; savor each dish,
    But never fear a delicious wish.

They pipe up, telling stories anew,
"Never trust a cat, they'll trick you!"
For wisdom lives with a playful twist,
And in every heart, there's joy to list.

So gather round as they share their lore,
"Count the laughs; you'll always score!"
    Generations pass, humor entwined,
    An endless circle, forever aligned.

Illuminations of Insight

Light bulbs flicker in those wrinkled minds,
"Don't chase after cars; they don't have pines!"
Through quirky wisdom, the truth is shown,
In jests and chuckles, the seeds are sown.

"Don't put all your eggs in one small coop!"
A reminder to dance, not just to stoop!
For through the laughter, lessons will drip,
Life's a wild and whimsical trip.

They spin tales of mishaps and cheer,
"Wrestle with life, never with fear!"
In each little giggle, a light is found,
Wisdom is playful, laughter unbound.

So as they chime with insightful glee,
"Live like a frog, jump joyfully!"
Let the glow of humor lead your way,
In these illuminations, we choose to stay.

Fragments of Foresight

A penny saved is a penny earned,
But where's the penny that I spurned?
They say to save for rainy days,
    But I prefer to ride the rays.

If life gives lemons, make a pie,
Lemonade's too mainstream, oh my!
The road less traveled's often rough,
    But I prefer my path to be fluff.

If at first you do not succeed,
Just blame it on a bad breed.
Failure's just a friend in disguise,
Who juggles lessons without lies.

So keep your fork, it's dessert time,
Eatin' pudding is always prime.
With laughter echoing through the halls,
    Wisdom's fun when it gently calls.

Notes from the Ancient

Old scrolls remind us not to fret,
A cat can pounce, but dogs forget.
The ancient wisdom, so out of hand,
Might just need a little band.

A wise man once spilled his tea,
Said life's just chaos, can't you see?
When doors close tight with a bang,
It's a chance for a silly slang.

Season your words, sprinkle with cheer,
A dash of fun brings wisdom near.
For every sage who sat so still,
There's a jester laughing on the hill.

So write your truths but scribble a joke,
A giggle sprinkles 'round the cloak.
In ancient scripts so bright and bold,
Let laughter be the tales retold.

Beacons of Perspective

When clouds bring shadows, just wear shades,
Perspective flips like silly parades.
A lighthouse stands with a beam so wide,
That only the clueless choose to hide.

The wise man's beard, a tangled maze,
Supposedly hides all the old days.
But secrets have a way to flee,
With a tickle and a cup of tea.

One spoon of sugar, a sprinkle of zest,
Turns frowns to smiles, it's truly the best.
So put on your glasses, flip the script,
Find humor in woes that often slip.

A wobbly chair and a sneaky cat,
Are symbols of wisdom, imagine that!
With each laugh shared like a bright spark,
Life's funny quotes create the mark.

The Way of the Mindful

They say to breathe and don't be dense,
Yet yoga twists seem quite immense.
One foot in front, please do not fall,
Mindful moments make us all tall.

A mindful snack? Just don't you dare,
Crunching chips while on a chair.
For every chip you take and munch,
Remember, it's wise to have a bunch.

Meditation's great for finding peace,
But falling asleep is quite the release.
The mantra of the still night air,
Is finding joy in a comfy chair.

So live each day with a wink and cheer,
Mindfulness can mean a little beer.
Laugh through the chaos, keep it bright,
For the way of fun is truly right.

Piecing Together the Past

Old photographs pile up high,
Telling tales as time drifts by.
Grandma's stories, quite absurd,
Like the time she lost a bird!

Memory's puzzle, what a laugh,
Found my socks, lost my path!
History's secrets in the attic,
Also a cat that's aromatic!

Digging deep, I find my shoe,
Beneath old books, it lost its cue.
Every corner holds a jest,
Life's confusion is the best!

Pieces fit, though not quite right,
A comedy in faded light.
With each glance, I burst with glee,
Past and present shaping me!

Wisdom on the Wind

Whispers float from leaves so green,
Drawing laugh lines, quite unseen.
A butterfly snickers, takes flight,
On advice that feels just right.

Clouds drift by with quiet grace,
Making faces in the space.
If laughter's breeze can guide the day,
Then let's just dance and twist away!

Old man craves a quiet day,
Hearing gales that laugh and sway.
"Life's a riddle," he will chime,
With the wind, we skip on time!

Every gust a lesson clear,
Blowing past our doubt and fear.
So hear the chuckles, wild and free,
In every rustle, there's humor to see!

The Compass of Convictions

Navigating life's odd seas,
With a compass that just teases.
Pointing north, then south with glee,
Telling tales of where to be!

Follow your gut, it grumbles loud,
But that's just hunger, not a crowd.
Taste of wisdom, spicy, hot,
Maybe ignore the strange, you knot!

Directions change with every rhyme,
But that's okay, we've got the time.
Flip a coin, let fate decide,
Though I may end up quite outside!

With each twist and turn I make,
I find my joys in every mistake.
So here's to maps and quirky plans,
Let's laugh together, life's in our hands!

Gathered Under the Old Oak

Beneath the oak, we share our tales,
Of childhood dreams and silly fails.
Branching out, the laughter spreads,
As wisdom tumbles from our heads.

Squirrels steal our snacks with flair,
Cheeky rogues, they do not care!
"Stealing wisdom," someone grins,
"Must be why they always win!"

The roots, they twist like our delight,
Entanglements, both wrong and right.
Circle round, the stories grow,
Each giggle adds to the show!

As sun sets down and stars appear,
We toast to all our laughter here.
Under the oak, life seems so grand,
With echoes of joy, hand in hand!

The Map of Memory

When lost in thought, remember this,
A map's just lines, a treasure's bliss.
Your mind can wander, twist and turn,
But finding gold, we all still yearn.

Each path you take, a chance to find,
A snippet sweet, a laugh unkind.
So mark your spots with laughter's ink,
And share the tales without a wink.

Mistakes are markers, don't you fret,
They guide you well, no regrets yet.
With every wrong, a lesson dear,
Just hug your quirks, and dry your tear.

So bring your compass, true and bold,
In memory's land, there's treasure untold.
A journey's fun when we play the fool,
With giggles and glee, it's the heart's true jewel.

Navigating the Waters of Experience

In life's wide ocean, boats drift and sway,
With humor as sails, we'll find our way.
The waves may crash, but we'll shout and sing,
For a wet, wild ride can be a great thing.

Each splash a lesson, each gust a cheer,
Forget the map—just steer with good beer!
Choppy waters may make you blunder,
But laughter's the raft that keeps you from under.

With fishy tales and stories tall,
Jokes about sinking will make you enthrall.
If you see a shark, just wink and shout,
"Swim, you fishy, I'm not out!"

So set sail boldly into the blue,
Trust your gut, it knows what to do.
With every wave, a giggle or two,
Navigating life can be quite the zoo.

Cadences of Clarity

In the rhythm of life, a beat goes on,
Sometimes it's jazz, sometimes it's a con.
When things get muddy, just tap your toe,
Move to the sound, let funny flows grow.

Clear the fog with a chuckle or cheer,
Grab a banjo, a ukulele, or beer.
The more you laugh, the clearer it gets,
Don't fret the rhythm; it's filled with bets.

Dance through mistakes with a silly song,
Each misstep notes where you still belong.
In a symphony, we all find a part,
Humor's the tune that warms every heart.

So strum your way through life's quirky path,
With giggles and grins, dodge the math.
For in the end, it's not just a race,
But a sweet serenade that sets the pace.

Voices of the Veiled

Behind every curtain, a secret lies,
With whispers of laughter, and joyful sighs.
Don your disguise with a wink and a grin,
For life's little dramas are where we begin.

Each masked encounter, a chuckle or two,
With jesters and fools, we dance into view.
From shadows to spotlight, we play our role,
In a world of illusion, we find the whole.

So when life gets awkward, just lean into cheers,
Let the voices of joy drown out the fears.
For with every mask, a story awaits,
A tale wrapped in giggles, the best of fates.

So peek through the veil and spread the delight,
Join the ruckus, turn darkness to light.
In a carnival of quirks, come join the parade,
Where every odd voice shines, joyfully played.

Guardians of the Gist

In the land of snorts and giggles bright,
Wise ones dance in the moonlight.
They say, "A jest will often save,
A fool's pride, a wise man's grave!"

With a wink, they toss a thought,
"Don't think too hard; that's how you're caught!"
Laughter echoes, a joyous ring,
A light heart can't help but sing!

They hand out tips like candy sprinkles,
"Life's too short for fretful crinkles!"
One's misstep makes another's day,
While mishaps dance and play away!

So heed the giggles in your chest,
In laughter, find your very best.
Among the wise, be quick to jest,
The world is bright; be not a pest!

The Light of Laughter and Learning

With a chuckle and a wink, they say,
"There's wisdom found in blissful play!"
Each giggle holds a hint of truth,
Light on worry, heavy on youth!

A riddle we've all heard before,
"Why did the chicken cross the floor?"
To teach the fool to take a chance—
And maybe learn a funny dance!

Ponder not in heavy streams,
For life's a joke, or so it seems.
Twist your brain with laughter's light,
And watch your troubles take to flight!

So join the jesters on the stage,
Where wisdom wears a funny age.
In light of laughter, learn to grin,
For wisdom thrives where fun begins!

Words Woven in Time

Once was a wise guy with a sock,
His words would laugh, his humor rock!
"If life hands you lemons, make a drink,
And offer one to those who think!"

Knots of knowledge, twisted with glee,
Like a clown with a splash of tea.
"Get it wrong but do it loud,
For silence lives beneath the crowd!"

As they spun tales of slip and trip,
Life's absurdities took a dip.
"A joke well-timed beats all advice,
So add a wink, and roll the dice!"

Their wisdom like a playful breeze,
Bringing laughter with joyful ease.
In life's tapestry, woven tight,
Funny threads shine all the bright!

Of Stars and Wisdom

Look up to see the shining stars,
Whispering tales of life's bizarre.
"When in doubt, just laugh it through,
Life's a circus, and you're the zoo!"

The wise ones speak in riddles spry,
"Why reach for the moon when you can fly?"
Twinkle, twinkle, guide our plight,
In silliness, we find our light!

With each cosmic chuckle shared,
The universe reveals it cared.
A burst of giggles from the skies,
With laughter, let your spirit rise!

So gather round, embrace the fun,
Life's a game that's never done.
In the starlit humor, be adrift,
For wisdom bloomed is life's best gift!

Chronicles of Knowledge

In a book, I found a phrase,
It said, 'Don't eat that soup too hot!'
But when I tried, my tongue went blaze,
Now I'm known as the lad who forgot!

Wisdom tells us to be discreet,
Especially when it comes to eats.
'Procrastinate tomorrow' it's fleet,
Yet here I am, still in my seats!

A wise old man once did declare,
'Life's too short for second-hand socks.'
Yet here I stand, with mismatched flair,
It's all the rage, or so says the flocks!

So take your wisdom, hold it tight,
But laugh a little, don't take flight.
For in the end, when day turns to night,
We're all just chasing the same delight!

Threads of Tradition

Gather 'round, dear kin and friends,
And listen to the tales well-spun.
Once they said, 'Time's a river that bends,'
Now I just think it's out for fun.

They taught us to dance and twirl,
But forgot to mention the pitfalls too.
So here I am, my feet in a whirl,
While Auntie laughs — she knows what's new!

Tradition says to pass the pie,
But always keep the crumbs at bay.
"It's just dessert!" I hear them sigh,
Oops, that was my new shirt today!

In every story, there's a twist,
Lessons learned with a hearty laugh.
Cherish the moments, none to miss,
Life's a joke — cut it in half!

The Light of Learning

They say that knowledge is a flame,
It lights the path, or so they say.
But here I fumble, what a shame,
My candle's melting — hey, don't stray!

In classes bright, our minds ignite,
With facts and figures all around.
Yet when I quiz, it's such a fright,
My brain's a circus — clowns abound!

One sage proclaimed, 'To learn is fun,'
But homework feels like climbing cliffs.
Just when I thought I'd seen the sun,
The math went wild with crazy shifts!

But laughter's spark can light the day,
In every lesson, find the jest.
With jokes and joy, we'll pave the way,
So come and learn, it's for the best!

Enigmas from the Eld

Old tales whisper through the trees,
With riddles wrapped in mystery's shroud.
"What is the sound of a bee with fleas?"
I scratched my head — oh, wisdom's loud!

An elder said, "Avoid the rush,
Take life as slow as a molasses snail."
But here I am, in a frantic hush,
I'd rather zoom like a speedy trail!

"When in doubt, just wear bright socks,"
One wise one winked with a knowing smile.
But all I got were sideways knocks,
Now I'm a fashion faux pas for a while!

Through puzzles shared, and laughter loud,
The gems of life begin to shine.
Embrace the quirks, stand up with pride,
For in the jest, our truths align!

Timely Reminders

Don't count your chickens, they won't lay,
Numbers can lie, much to dismay.
If you trip on a shoelace, just laugh it away,
Life's just a game, so go out and play.

Never judge a book by its worn cover,
That old mystery might be just a lover.
Coffee spills happen, don't be a griever,
Just call it art, you aspiring achiever.

A watched pot never seems to boil,
But a daydream can make the heart uncoil.
Whistle while you work, let joy uncoil,
And dance in the rain, let life's funsoil!

If it ain't broke, don't fix it too soon,
Trust in the rhythm, like a merry tune.
Lemons can make a pie, not just a frown,
Wear mismatched socks, strut all over town!

Heritages of the Heart

In this family tree, we're all a bit strange,
Great Aunt Edna talks to chairs, it's deranged.
Uncle Joe wears socks with sandals, no change,
But love's the thread that keeps us allanged.

Mom's recipe for chaos is deliciously bold,
Burnt toast and laughter, a sight to behold.
Grab a fork, who cares about the mold?
Her tales are treasures more precious than gold.

Dad claims he's an expert in juggling socks,
But we just roll our eyes and hide our clocks.
He'll say, 'It's all in the wrist!' – oh, the schlocks,
Yet each joyful moment is worth all the knocks.

Embrace the quirks, let the smiles grow,
In our little world, we steal quite a show.
Life's a dance, and we're all in the flow,
We'll twirl through the oddities, come rain or snow!

Bottled Reflections

A penny saved is just a penny, right?
But sometimes it's fun to splurge on a bite.
Fish may swim, but don't take flight,
Just keep your swim trunks and your laughter tight.

Chasing dreams is like herding cats,
They run off fast, and regardless of chats.
Dance like no one's watching, in silly hats,
And laugh out loud, it's where joy's at.

Mirror, mirror, what do you see?
A person who's trying, and that's enough glee.
Fences may limit, but hearts stay free,
In this wild world, be your own jam spree.

Hide your quirks in plain sight, oh please,
Life's a comedy, so let's not tease.
Pop the cork and let the fun increase,
In bottled reflections, find your peace!

Verities in Verses

Truth can be silly, take it from me,
Like socks on a chicken or a dancing flea.
Let laughter ring out like a joyful decree,
In the realm of the absurd, we're all fancy-free.

Two wrongs don't make a right, so they say,
But what if they twirl and dance their own way?
Join the conga line, don't be led astray,
Life's just a series of funny ballet.

Share your wisdom with a side of fun,
Like a quirky family play starring everyone.
Quotes can rhyme, and they should run,
In this grand circus, we're all number one.

So claim your truths, don't take it too grim,
Laugh at the quirks, and dance on a whim.
With a smile as your coat, life's not so dim,
Verities in verses, let the joy brim!

Whispers of Wisdom

In the thick of a crowd, one voice did shout,
"Always keep your head high, even when you pout!"
Global wisdom wrapped in a jest,
Laughter's the trick, forget all the rest.

A cat on a fence, with a very wise grin,
Said, "Life's like a box of fish — just dive right in!"
When the referee's blind, and you own the court,
Just remember, my friend, life's still a sport!

So dance to the tune of a silly old frog,
And juggle those lemons, don't walk like a cog.
For the punchline of life, trust the giggling gnome,
When lost on your path, just follow the foam.

With candy-coated truths bouncing off the walls,
Hear the giggles of wisdom in these funny halls.
So grab a light heart and a chuckle or two,
For wisdom is fun, like a joke just for you.

Echoes of Enlightenment

A wise old owl sat upon a tree,
"Count your jumping beans, and then you'll be free!"
Twiddling his feathers and casting a glance,
Life's a great circus, so join in the dance!

When the goat says 'Moo' and the cow says 'Neigh',
You know something's cooking, don't look the other way!

With wisdom like pudding, all creamy and bright,
Mix in the laughter, and it'll feel just right.

So listen to whispers from under the bed,
There's treasure in giggles, not just in your head.
The shoe that you lost, well, it's just having fun,
It's probably dancing under the moon and sun!

As bubbles of thought float around in the night,
Embrace the absurd, it's all pure delight.
So chatter with shadows and tickle your fate,
In the echo of laughter, find time to create.

Threads of Thought

A goldfish once said, with a glint in its eye,
"You swim in your bowl, but you can still fly!"
Life's a fine tapestry, woven by clowns,
Where giggles are kings and the grumps wear frowns.

When socks go missing, just send out a prayer,
They're partying hard with the dust bunnies there.
The spoon that won't stir, well, it knows its own way,
It dances with fame at the bottom of fray.

With wisdom as sticky as honey on toast,
Let your laughter grow loud and be proud of your boast!
For every wise quote that hangs on your wall,
Wait for the punchline — it's the best part of all!

In threads of thought, where fun intertwines,
You'll find wisdom hiding, playing in lines.
So tug at those strings, let the fun begin,
For laughter's the key, let the joy flow in!

The Quiet Truths

In a garden of quirks where the daisies all chat,
"Beware of the wisecracks, they bite like a cat!"
A dandelion whispered, with a giggle so spry,
"Truth's like my seeds, it just wants to fly!"

The snail with a backpack, all ready to roam,
Said, "Take it slow, but do bring your foam!"
With secrets hidden under a unicycle's wheel,
The quietest truths often squeal with appeal.

So dance with the fireflies and twirl in the air,
Life's just a riddle, don't you dare declare!
For every dusty bookshelf and wise old sage,
There's laughter in the lines, like a playful page.

In the stillness of moments, where giggles reside,
The quietest truths make the wildest ride.
So breathe in the charm, let the smiles unfurl,
With humor as your compass, explore this great whirl!

Lessons Etched in Memory

When life gives you lemons, grab some gin,
Mix up a joke, let the laughter begin.
A wise man once tripped over his pride,
Said, 'I bounce back; I won't be denied!'

Fortune favors those who can laugh,
At mishaps that come, like a photograph.
So write down your blunders, frame them well,
In a gallery where humor will dwell.

The road to wisdom is paved with smirks,
And often travels through comical quirks.
Remember, the past is a riotous book,
With every slip-up, in laughter we look.

When wisdom's around, don't take it too hard,
A chuckle's the shield, laughter's the guard.
Each lesson a giggle, each mistake a grin,
In the art of living, here's where we win!

The Counsel of Clouds

Clouds drift above, with tales to tell,
They laugh and they cry, but all's well.
One old cloud said, 'Don't take life too strict,
When it rains, just dance—it's all a trick!'

If thunder rolls in, don't hide in your bed,
It just wants to play, not strike you dead.
So twirl like a leaf, be silly, be loud,
You'll be wiser, believe, from the heart of a cloud.

Every fluffy shape holds wisdom in flight,
A whale, a dog, or a giant delight.
Listen closely, their giggles abound,
For joy drifts along with a floaty sound.

So next time you gaze at sky's grand display,
Remember its laughter as you go play.
Let the wind tell stories, both bright and absurd,
In nature's grand theater, be hopeful and heard!

Pearls of Understanding

Life's pearls are found in the oddest of places,
Like crumbs on your shirt, in forgotten embraces.
One wise guy with socks that don't match,
Said, 'If you trip, just start a new catch!'

Listen closely, there's wisdom in gaffes,
A barrel of laughs in life's wobbly halves.
A wise owl hoots, 'Don't sweat the small stuff,
Laugh at the mishaps; they're really just fluff!'

Grab every chuckle, it's worth a gold coin,
In awkwardness lies the joys that we join.
Life's lessons are nuggets, unearthed through the jest,
So wear that smile, and let silence rest.

With each quirky moment, you gather the light,
Understanding's a dance, not just black and white.
Keep those pearls close, in laughter they gleam,
And learn from the follies; it's a wonderful dream!

Folklore of the Heart

In every old tale, there's a twist to the plot,
Like a cat who can't swim, or a pig that can trot.
A wisecrack once woke in a grand old chair,
Said, 'Life's but a ride on a whimsical air!'

Every heart has a story, a laugh, and a plea,
Like dancing with shadows by the shade of a tree.
A leaky old boat may just float in a laugh,
Delightful mishaps are life's little gaffs.

Oh, the folklore spins! With a twist and a grin,
The fool wears the crown; let the laughter begin.
Climb trees with old friends, or jump in a bog,
In tales of the heart, we dance like a frog.

So grab your cap, let's venture afar,
For each joke's a beacon, a guiding star.
In the plot of our lives, we'll write what we feel,
With humor as ink, our stories are real.

www.ingramcontent.com/pod-product-compliance
Lightning Source LLC
Chambersburg PA
CBHW072149200426
43209CB00051B/927